SPOTLIGHT ON
AN EQUITABLE WORLD

CHOOSING RESPECT

Mary Ratzer

ROSEN PUBLISHING

Published in 2025 by The Rosen Publishing Group, Inc.
2544 Clinton Street, Buffalo, NY 14224

First Edition

Editor: Greg Roza
Book Design: Michael Flynn

Photo Credits: Cover Ground Picture/Shutterstock.com; cover, p. 3 (hands) Dedraw Studio/Shutterstock.com; (series Earth icon) v4ndhira/Shutterstock.com; p. 5 CREATISTA/Shutterstock.com; p. 6 cdrin/Shutterstock.com; pp. 7, 23 fizkes/Shutterstock.com; p. 9 Adam Cole/Shutterstock.com; p. 10 miker/Shutterstock.com; p. 11 Jeff Bukowski/Shutterstock.com; p. 13 Katherine Welles/Shutterstock.com; p. 14 Peter Rhys Williams/Shutterstock.com; p. 15 https://commons.wikimedia.org/wiki/File:Frederik_de_Klerk_with_Nelson_Mandela_-_World_Economic_Forum_Annual_Meeting_Davos_1992.jpg; pp. 17, 21, 27 Monkey Business Images/Shutterstock.com; p. 18 Konstantin Chagin/Shutterstock.com; p. 22 Sabphoto/Shutterstock.com; p. 25 Rawpixel.com/Shutterstock.com; p. 26 FrankHH/Shutterstock.com; p. 29 Pressmaster/Shutterstock.com.

Cataloging-in-Publication Data

Names: Ratzer, Mary Boyd.
Title: Choosing respect / Mary Ratzer.
Description: Buffalo, NY : Rosen Young Adult, 2025. | Series: Spotlight on an equitable world | Includes glossary and index.
Identifiers: ISBN 9781499477313 (pbk.) | ISBN 9781499477207 (library bound) | ISBN 9781499477047 (ebook)
Subjects: LCSH: Respect--Juvenile literature. | Respect for persons--Juvenile literature. | Courtesy--Juvenile literature. | Conduct of life--Juvenile literature.
Classification: LCC BJ1533.R4 R38 2025 | DDC 179'.9--dc23

Manufactured in the United States of America

Some of the images in this book illustrate individuals who are models. The depictions do not imply actual situations or events.

CPSIA Compliance Information: Batch #CSRYA25. For further information contact Rosen Publishing at 1-800-237-9932.

CONTENTS

Chapter One

DEFINING RESPECT

What does "respect" mean to you? A high school Respect Club used the morning announcements to ask this very question. The classic song by Aretha Franklin resounded through the building: "R-E-S-P-E-C-T! Find out what it means to me!" After introducing the club to the school, members and their allies shared the meaning of respect during meetings to build a safe and positive school climate. They learned from each other, from their other peers, and from teachers.

Respect is the foundation for building a positive school community. Giving respect and getting respect lead to two different perspectives. Adolescents are aware of getting respect from teachers, peers, and adults in their lives. Being respected is a big part of status and belonging. A diverse group of middle school students shared the idea that when your peers respect you, you respect them. Giving respect gets respect.

Adolescents have been taught respectful attitudes. The word "should" comes up often. Students talk about respecting authority, doing what they are told, and honoring military or first responders with respect. Some teens believe that all people should be respected because they are human beings. Giving respect because you should is different from giving respect because you care.

Adolescents understand respect with their heads and feel it in their hearts. Respect based on feelings from within is a response linked to empathy. A positive attitude and the choice to give respect builds relationships and communities. Respect can become a mindset or way of relating to others. Respect can mean that a fundamental positive attitude toward people and even things drives positive decisions and responses.

To many young people, respect is kindness, helping someone, or caring. Making sure a peer is OK is also respect.

Chapter Two

RESPECTING DIFFERENCES

The Greater Good Science Center at the University of California, Berkeley, explores well-being. The staff teaches skills that support health, happiness, and positive connections with other people. These skills foster successful human beings who can make the world a better place. The center focuses on bridging differences and building diverse social connections.

Adolescents often choose friends who are similar to them. Youth find it easy to show respect to others who share their age, gender identity, race, ethnicity, and religion. Forming friendships outside of this comfortable circle can be challenging. The safety and comfort of belonging to a group makes friendships outside the closed circle seem risky.

UNIVERSITY OF CALIFORNIA, BERKELEY CAMPUS

Everyone deserves respect in the community, regardless of their background, abilities, gender identity, age, or ethnicity.

The Greater Good Science Center partnered with the organization EL Education to interview middle school students about respect, and many mentioned respecting people who were different from them. Their responses showed awareness and a positive perspective: "Respect means to respect other people's culture and don't judge them by their food, their clothes, or what they wear," one said. It was important to another student that respect involve another's "culture, or race, their beliefs, and their traditions." Yet another student said that respect was important because "everyone has different rights and traditions." These comments reflect open-mindedness, which is needed to foster respect.

In an increasingly diverse society, young people encounter differences more than ever. Youth who have awareness and acceptance of both similarities and differences can empathize with others and value fairness. Developing moral principles and broader perspectives helps youth to be open to and accepting of differences. Friendships between diverse adolescents and positive views about differences lead to respect.

Chapter Three

SELF-RESPECT AND RESPECT

Self-respect communicates confidence and character to those around you. Self-respect is positive proof of your worth and abilities. When you believe in your right to fairness, self-respect carries your words and actions forward. Self-respect can be heard in your voice. It can be seen in your determination. Self-respect can earn you the respect of others. It can move those who are in the wrong or acting unfairly to change their minds.

Every spring, Native American students from across the country contact the Native American Rights Fund for support and advocacy. Schools in many states will not allow Native American graduates to wear tribal or religious symbols with their caps and gowns. These schools limit Native American liberty. Native students have to choose between participating in graduation with their classmates or following their cultural traditions.

Kamryn Yanchick was hopeful when she graduated high school in 2018 that she could honor her Native American heritage by decorating her cap with a beaded pattern. Kamryn is a citizen of the Seminole Nation of Oklahoma. Her Oklahoma high school administrators told her no. Kamryn hopes Oklahoma joins legislatures in nearly 12 states that have heard the voices of Native students and supported court decisions. They have passed laws to protect the rights of Native students to freely practice their religion and free speech in their schools.

It can be important for graduating high school students to show their connection to Native culture during graduation ceremonies because much of Native culture celebrates becoming an adult.

Native students believe in wearing meaningful cultural symbols at graduation. Eagle feathers, for example, represent self-respect and strength, wisdom, power, and freedom. This is a case in which self-respect can earn the respect of others.

Chapter Four

MASCOTS, STATUES, AND RESPECT

Teens who are active citizens can be leaders who help communities to choose respect over disrespect. A combination of awareness, questioning, and readiness to step up can launch community action for respect. In a variety of places and circumstances, teen involvement made change happen with mascots, statues, and place names in their communities.

There's a long, continuing debate in the United States over high school sports mascots based on stereotypes of Native American people. A database created by the National Council of American Indians recently identified almost 2,000 such mascots in U.S. schools. Progress often is credited to teens who found their way to active citizenship. Some teens are using social media to create change. Lily Joy Winder

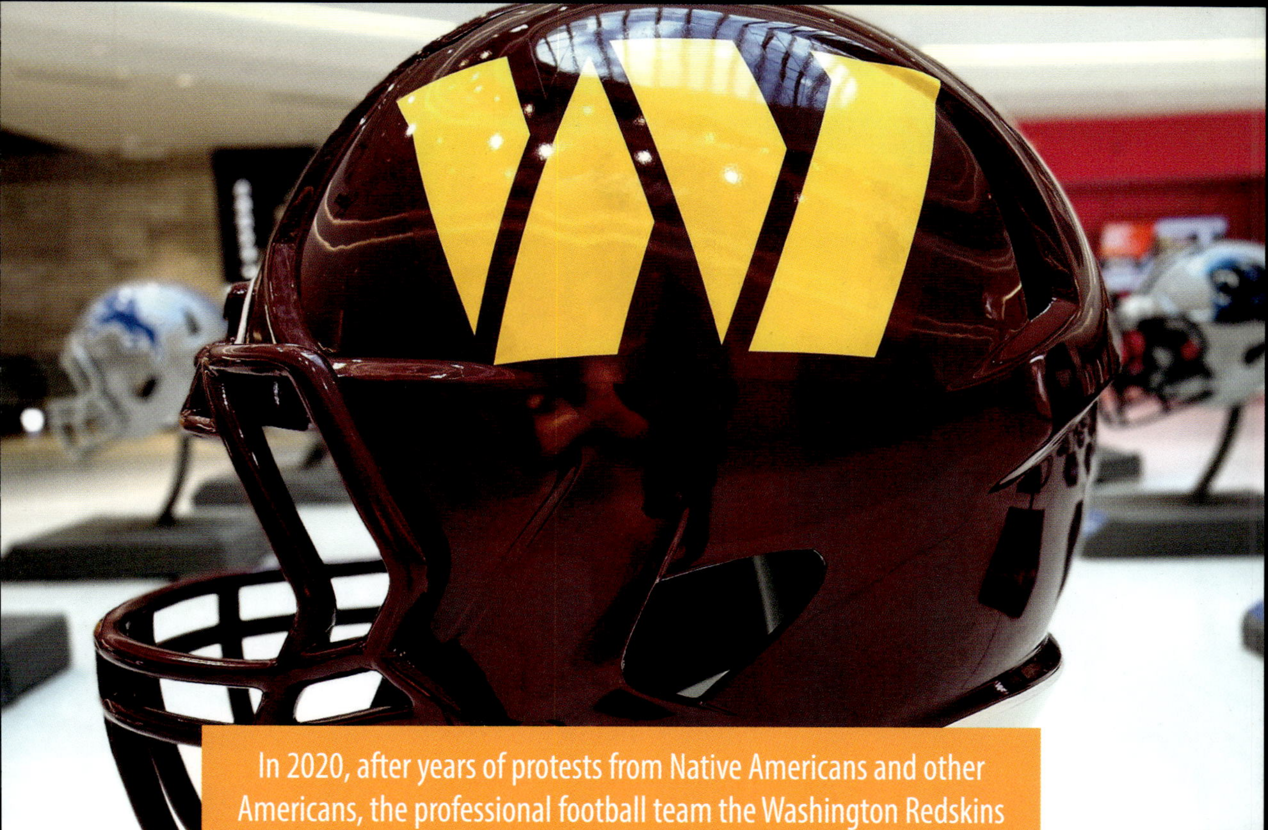

In 2020, after years of protests from Native Americans and other Americans, the professional football team the Washington Redskins finally changed their name to one that wasn't offensive to Native Americans. They are now called the Washington Commanders.

from Albuquerque, New Mexico, is one example. She became a Navajo (Diné) activist as a high school junior after creating TikTok videos to promote removing Native mascots from U.S. high schools. She has gained hundreds of thousands of followers.

Native teens who encounter the stereotyped mascots often feel a loss of human dignity. Teens in Albany, New York, participated in a community effort seeking respect. A statue of a famous Albany Revolutionary War hero, Philip Schuyler, stood in the center of the city. The history of slavery during this time reveals that Schuyler was a slaveholder. The high school students helped to have the statue moved because of Schuyler's disrespect for enslaved Africans. Efforts like these from concerned teens help make positive changes.

Chapter Five

MAKING CHANGES FOR RESPECT

A high school in Moore County, North Carolina, gained national attention by solving a dilemma with respect. Many monuments in the South were established to honor Civil War military leaders. They are reminders of racism and the institution of slavery. An auditorium in Pinecrest High School hosted music events for the school's bands, orchestras, and choruses. In 1992, it was named the Robert E. Lee Auditorium.

Many in the community supported this dedication because it honored a school district superintendent who fought to desegregate the schools in his county. His name was Robert E. Lee. Also known as Bob Lee, he unified Black schools and white schools, building a large, new facility. He desegregated the schools long before many others and faced opposing citizens.

For 30 years, young Black students felt fear and disrespect seeing the Robert E. Lee Auditorium as they came on campus. A junior who believed that the auditorium's true namesake should be known worked with other students to create and share a documentary about the superintendent Robert E. Lee and the auditorium. A Black student in the Pinecrest Speech and Debate Club narrated it. The video was shared with the student body on the last day of school.

Near the end of the video, Superintendent Lee's son and daughter are asked about changing the auditorium's name to avoid confusion. They both seem open to ideas such as Bob Lee or R.E. Lee Auditorium.

This statue of Robert E. Lee, the Confederate military leader, was removed from a park in Charlottesville, Virginia, in 2021. It's one of many statues that have been torn down because they can be seen as supporting the South's past racist practice of slavery.

Chapter Six

UBUNTU MEANS RESPECT

Many cultures of the world have inspiring ideas about respect. One idea helped to heal a racially divided nation. The harsh racist government of South Africa enforced laws that separated Blacks from whites from 1948 to 1994. This system made life separate and not equal based on race. Poverty, loss of rights, and restrictions on many aspects of life were parts of apartheid. In 1991, when Nelson Mandela and the white President F.W. de Klerk negotiated an end to apartheid, South Africa finally found a path to healing.

Bishop Desmond Tutu spoke of healing after the strife of apartheid. He spoke of an African tribal belief called Ubuntu. Bishop Tutu knew that only forgiveness and humanity could let people live in peace together. Being a part of humanity means being respectful of all.

BISHOP DESMOND TUTU

After many years in prison for his anti-apartheid stance, Nelson Mandela was released by new president F.W. de Klerk. Together, Mandela and de Klerk worked to end apartheid for good.

Belonging to the community means living respectfully. These are his words about Ubuntu:

"Those who had Ubuntu were compassionate and gentle, they used their strength on behalf of the weak, and they did not take advantage of others—in short, they cared, treating others as what they were: human beings. If you lacked Ubuntu, in a sense you lacked an … ingredient of being human."

Ubuntu goes further in its connections between being human and respect for others. It means thriving and uplifting together. The differences that could separate people include gifts that are needed by others. People depend on one another and their varied gifts. To be human is to be dependent on others and to use your gifts for others.

Chapter Seven

TEACHERS AND RESPECT

Adolescents learn more easily when they feel heard, understood, and cared about. They are keenly aware of when adults are treating them with respect and when they aren't. Teens engage with adults who respect them. Even as they move toward independence, their choice to engage with respectful teachers promotes learning. Students experience a sense of well-being in a respectful learning environment and can more easily find respect.

What does respect look like to adolescents in school? Teachers who challenge their students and move them out of their comfort zone respect the potential of their learners. High standards along with support when needed feel like respect in the classroom. Students feel respected when adults accept their beliefs and values, even when they are different. Respect involves teachers listening and responding to students without judgment. Respectful teachers have genuine concern for their students' well-being, and they recognize and respond to their students' needs. Respectful teachers value their students and communicate that.

Respect is built on students having choices and a chance to develop decision-making skills. Giving students a say in classroom culture and meaningful learning shows respect. Rules decided by a teacher and handed down without explanation do not encourage student engagement. Students making decisions results in their ownership of learning and motivation to succeed. Relationships developed between teachers and learners can support growth and model respectful connections with others. Caring and encouragement can bring out the best in struggling learners. Students can see themselves through the respectful eyes of their teachers.

Teachers can teach their students about respect by showing respect for their students.

Chapter Eight

PROGRAMS TO OPEN RESPECTFUL MINDS

No One Eats Alone Day (NOEA) is a day of action that encourages youth to sit with others, find new friends, and model ways to end social isolation in the lunchroom. Focusing on middle school students, the program engages kids at a time when isolation is a damaging common reality. Annually, over 2,500 schools participate in NOEA, reaching over 1,000,000 students.

You can learn more about 24/7 Respect by viewing the video online. Starring teens from the Boston public school system, this video offers viewers a number of scenarios and asks them to explain why a situation might be considered unfair or disrespectful.

Sandy Hook Promise Programs value the protection of children. Motivated by the 2012 school shooting in Newtown, Connecticut, Sandy Hook Promise creates national programs for schools and communities. They organize the following initiatives:

- **Start with Hello Week** encourages youth nationwide to expand their social connections and to help others find a sense of belonging.
- **Students Against Violence Everywhere (SAVE) Promise Club** is a youth leadership initiative. Led by a youth advisory board, the aim is to empower young leaders to take an active role in increasing school safety and preventing different forms of violence.
- **Know the Signs** programs teach youth and adults how to prevent school violence, spot behaviors that can lead to violence, and know how to take action to get help.
- **Say Something** programs teach students how to recognize the warning signs of someone at risk of hurting themselves or others, and how to get help.

24/7 Respect is made up of students in grades 6 through 12 in Boston, Massachusetts. They show and discuss the video "24/7 Respect" to better understand how to identify and report bias-based misconduct. This fosters a safe, respectful, and welcoming environment.

Give Respect, Get Respect is an anti-bias program connecting middle and high school students, school leaders, and workers at local businesses to address diversity and encourage respect and acceptance. Students become leaders in their schools, challenging barriers that prevent students from connecting with each other.

Chapter Nine

BIAS AND THE BRAIN

Bias often involves your brain taking shortcuts or making mistakes. Bias and stereotypes are stories you accept about people before you know them. A stereotype means that people belonging to a group all have the same traits or characteristics in the mind of a biased person. The human brain looks for shortcuts and patterns, sometimes judging groups of people using stereotypes.

Often you are not aware of common causes for unfair judgments and attitudes. Influences that lead to bias are all around you. They include family attitudes, media, news, and images. New information about a group often makes no difference. A quick reflection on why you judged someone may not reveal your biased attitudes. Biases affect the way you think and act, but they are not on the surface.

One common shortcut the brain takes is judging people based on first impressions. This means that you do not know the person well or have any experience with them. You just meet the person and decide you do not like them for some reason. Or you could decide the person is fun and amazing, but you may have no idea about their personality, character, or values. Celebrities, famous athletes, and other public figures often only let the public see the part they are playing.

The human brain often pays more attention to the first thing it hears and backs away from the hard work of listening for a long time. Responsible decisions tend to take more work than snap judgments. Bias creeps into thinking because of influences that we just accept without realizing it.

Bullying can be based on biases, or beliefs about someone's social group. This social group can be related to one's race, religion, gender, color, or national origin.

Chapter Ten

THINK TWICE BEFORE YOU ACT

Sometimes, questions are the answer. Reflect on some questions that might lead to open-mindedness and respect for others. "How do I think about differences? Am I open-minded?" Reflecting on your own thinking is a powerful way to check in on bias. "How do I know about differences? What have I heard about a social group, an ethnicity, a religion? What are the sources of my attitudes and beliefs?"

Look at your experiences in the present. "Where do I see attitudes and behavior connected with stereotypes? Have I heard hate speech? Do my peers mock certain kids in the hallways or online? Do my jokes tap into biases and hurtful beliefs?" Stop and think twice! Filter your words and actions and reject those which are unfair.

As we have seen, there are many programs that reach out to teens and other community members to help reduce bias and increase mutual respect. However, it's good to look inward and ask yourself what you can do to be a better person to others.

Look at your past and how you grew up. Do you hold on to ideas shared by your identity group? Give them a second thought. Hold on to the beliefs and attitudes that influence your good character and values. Change your mind about beliefs and attitudes that have their roots in intolerance. You may not even realize that you have a bias that is a part of how you were raised.

Active listening is a powerful tool in being open-minded. With very personal and meaningful communication, keeping your focus is key to understanding and being understood. Barriers block understanding. You can learn to work through these barriers to listening when they turn up.

Chapter Eleven

I CAN!

Responsible decisions make you a part of the solution to problems of bias and unfairness. Making decisions based on your well-being and that of others is the first step in being a responsible person. Look carefully at the list of personal statements here. Decide if you can take responsible actions. Draw conclusions about goals you can set to be part of a caring and respectful community.

- **I can see the impact of my choices and goals on my community.**
- **I can have a role as a responsible and caring part of my community.**
- **I know I am connected to other people and can relate to them even when we are different or when we disagree.**
- **I build connections with other people by showing them empathy, respect, and understanding.**
- **I ask questions respectfully and listen carefully and nonjudgmentally.**
- **I can have problem-solving conversations about bias, unfairness, and hate.**
- **I know that biased words and behaviors affect the rights and freedoms of people.**
- **I can care about how people are treated and have empathy when they are mistreated because of their identities.**

You can share these statements with your friends. Together, you can work to make the world a better place.

- I know how to stand up for myself and for others when faced with unfairness and injustice.
- I can respectfully tell someone when their words or actions are biased or hurtful.
- I will speak up or act when I see unfairness, when it's safe and appropriate, and I will not let others convince me to go along with injustice.
- I will work with others to make our world fair.

Chapter Twelve

THE WORD "YES" AND RESPECT

First responders meet the needs of people in stressful and crisis situations. Meeting these needs requires caring for their physical and emotional well-being. An emergency room doctor in Visalia, California, Omar Guzman, realized that being stressed and overworked affected his relationships with his patients. He decided to bring respect into his work. Choosing to use empathy and to build relationships, he said yes to understanding, active listening, and respect.

A "Yes! And ..." attitude requires respecting and building on the ideas and input of others. This approach can help build mutual respect in a classroom. Saying yes to community-building activities breaks down barriers to relationships. Saying yes to opening a new connection with a peer can feel like a risk, but you can take it. You

Research has shown that when doctors show patients more empathy, patients tend to be better about following treatment plans and self-care practices.

are saying yes to stepping into a circle of connections that can build a community. You can be open to sharing who you are and growing your awareness about others. Once you say yes to that bridge, so many things change for the better.

By saying yes to new relationships and sharing, you learn as much about yourself as you do about others. Engaging with different types of people teaches you how to be a part of their world. Social awareness equips you to engage with those who are different from you. When many learners say yes to building their school community, success in schoolwork increases. Problems with a negative school climate decrease. Feeling that you are part of your school community reduces stress and builds safety and confidence.

Chapter Thirteen

BREAKING DOWN BIASES

Biases connect groups of people with negative qualities. Stereotypes often cause people to avoid contact with others who are different. Having new experiences with people who are different from you is the path to changing your mind. But avoiding a group blocks the opportunity to learn firsthand that stereotypes need to be dismissed. Awareness of your own biased ideas is the goal of the National Coalition Building Institute (NCBI). It's an international group that works with many schools.

The NCBI works with groups of students at many levels and trains them to become allies. Unlike other programs, the NCBI helps participants heal from guilt to combat negative attitudes, beliefs, stereotypes, and biases related to group identities such as gender, religion, and race.

During training, students who have encountered prejudice and discrimination volunteer to speak about their experiences. They describe being treated unfairly, being a target of hate speech, or facing biased judgment. Studies have shown that when people share stories about their experiences with bias or prejudice, they are more likely to change the attitudes that can lead to bias and discrimination. Often during NCBI trainings, participants are asked to reflect on their feelings about personal stories shared by group members.

Students with this training become allies and support individuals who are mistreated. They learn to take action to change unjust systems. They encourage others to help them or get involved.

The National Coalition Building Institute offers many workshops for K to 12 schools. One called "Welcoming Diversity—Building a Caring School Environment" focuses on building understanding and appreciation for differences among students and staff.

Chapter Fourteen

HAVING AN OPEN MIND

Practicing open-mindedness is not as easy as you might think. Being open to new ideas and new experiences means that you are actively paying attention to your thoughts. You are willing to listen, consider what is new, thoughtfully ask questions, and gather information for understanding. You are ready to use evidence to challenge your own beliefs. You think about what other people are thinking. Further, you are ready to change beliefs and attitudes that no longer work in your real world.

Open-minded people keep their curiosity alive and are able to have their ideas questioned by others. They work at keeping an empathetic attitude and believe that everyone has their own perspective. Communicating about diverse perspectives opens your mind and your world. Seeing all sides of an issue takes mental effort.

Even when conflicts arise, open-minded people listen to all sides, try to find common ground, and learn from mistakes. Listening is work, and it's so important in making open-mindedness work for you and others. Seeing things through the eyes of others makes compassion a valued response. Open-minded people are more likely to have a positive attitude, brush off hurtful words, and hold on to confidence.

Open-minded people benefit from their own fairness to others. Because they do not judge unfairly, they have fewer conflicts and less stress. Their relationships are based on acceptance and are both more positive and more diverse. Open-minded people learn from others and have rich experiences sharing with others. Friendships and connections affect happiness and mental health.

GLOSSARY

advocacy: The process or action of supporting a certain cause.

ally: One of two or more people or groups who work together.

desegregate: To end a policy that separates people of certain races.

dilemma: A situation that involves making a difficult, or hard, decision.

Diné: The term the Navajo people use to refer to themselves that translates in English to "The People."

discrimination: Unfairly treating people unequally because of their race or beliefs.

diverse: Made up of people who are different from one another.

empathy: A feeling that you comprehend and can share in another's experiences and emotions.

ethnicity: A certain ethnic group or affiliation. Ethnic is a term relating to large groups of people with certain racial, tribal, religious, linguistic, or cultural backgrounds.

gender identity: One's personal concept of themselves as a male, female, a blend of male and female, or neither gender. It can be the same or different from their birth-assigned sex.

heritage: The traditions and beliefs that are part of the history of a group or nation.

influence: An effect one thing has on another.

initiative: An act or strategy to improve a situation.

isolation: A state of being separated or apart from others.

perspective: A certain way of thinking about and comprehending a situation.

prejudice: An unfair feeling of dislike for a person or group because of race or religious or political beliefs.

stereotype: An often unfair and untrue belief people have about all members of a certain group.

strife: A disagreement between two or more people or groups that can be very violent or angry.

volunteer: To do something to help because you want to do it.

INDEX